CONTEMPORARY BRITISH ARTISTS:
WILLIAM ROTHENSTEIN
*General Editor:* ALBERT RUTHERSTON

SELF-PORTRAIT. (1899–1900). *Oil. Metropolitan Museum, New York.*

# WILLIAM ROTHENSTEIN

## LONDON: ERNEST BENN, LTD.
### 8 BOUVERIE STREET, E.C.4
1923

# ACKNOWLEDGMENT

THANKS are due to the National Gallery of British Art;
the National Gallery of Canada; the National
Gallery, Melbourne; the National Gallery, Johannesburg; the Metropolitan Museum, New York; and
the Imperial War Museum, for their kind permission
to reproduce works of which they own the Copyright.

Acknowledgment is gratefully offered also to those
private owners of Professor William Rothenstein's
work who have so courteously allowed it to be photo-
graphed for the purposes of this monograph, and to
Prof. Rothenstein himself for the valuable assist-
ance he has given.

Made and Printed in Great Britain at
*The Mayflower Press, Plymouth.* William Brendon & Son, Ltd.

# LIST OF PLATES

# LIST OF PLATES

# WILLIAM ROTHENSTEIN

IT was the fortune—or the fate—of William Rothenstein to appear early before the public as a " brilliant young man " in the somewhat self-conscious pages of the *Yellow Book* and the *Savoy*, and at the exhibitions of the New English Art Club, at a period when the Club was popularly supposed to exist only to expound the doctrine of " Art for Art's sake."

To commence exhibiting at twenty-one, to be noticed as a draughtsman in company with Beardsley and Conder, as a painter with Wilson Steer and Walter Sickert, as fellow wit with Max Beerbohm, and as a critical writer of challenging perspicacity while still in the twenties—this was to be alarmingly precocious and versatile. But to succeed, to attract serious attention in all these directions—what a dangerous position for any young man with long views upon art ! The later career of Mr. Rothenstein shows how real and solid were the foundations of talent and energy on which these beginnings were based, and how entirely he escaped being spoilt by his early success. It would be difficult to find an artist of his time more definitely self-controlled and purposeful in development, less swayed by either praise or criticism.

The art and literature of the eighteen-nineties, once decried as decadent, morbid, and perverse, have been rediscovered, and, with the enchantment lent by a distance of thirty years, have been hailed as peculiarly fascinating and romantic, though too often tragic in the early death or disablement of so many famous protagonists. Less extreme than either view is that given by Mr. Teixera de Mattos, who, writing from personal remembrance, described his friends of the nineties who were particularly " of the movement " as " a group of men, mostly under thirty, who just wrote and drew and painted as well as they could, in all sincerity and with no view to financial gain." There was, indeed, a danger, in the ideas of the period, especially to those working in the plastic arts. It lay in the defects inherent in their best qualities. In the revolt against the conventional subject picture, so much value was placed upon the exquisite and unusual that fastidious taste inclined to take the place of more robust creative power. " Quality not quantity " was a text worth remembering, and badly needed emphasising, and it was rightly felt that a delicate lithograph, dry point, or decorative title page, might well be more valuable than a ponderous gallery picture. Again, the decorative inventions of Beardsley

8

and Conder appeared amazingly pictorial and refreshing by contrast with banal and unselective copying of posed models. The appreciation of the special qualities of beauty inherent in every medium and the realisation that purely pictorial qualities, and a sense of style, were essential in a work of art, whether fantastic or realistic, were positive gains. Moreover, it was stimulating to discover an art which, however slight it might be, showed a personal and genuine sensibility to beauty. The danger lay in accepting taste rather than direct emotional or æsthetic experience, as a sufficient basis for creative activity, and in taking the slightness of some charming lithographs and water-colours on silk to be an end in itself.

Mr. Rothenstein was susceptible to all these interests of the period, but was carried beyond them by his immense interest in life, and in all forms of human activity that show intelligence and spirit. If " Art for Art's sake " had any meaning for him, it surely lay in the thoroughly healthy belief which every artist worth his salt must hold, that to him his particular art is the most important and valuable thing in life. Though Beardsley, Yeats, Arthur Symons, Max Beerbohm, Wilson Steer, Henry Harland, and Dowson were his friends, and though he actively took his share in the movement, Mr. Rothenstein could never be claimed as a slavish adherent to any special clique. His acutely critical mind was a considerable force in the New English Art Club, but he always kept his personal independence. As early as 1900 his scholarly monograph on Goya contained such affirmations as the following, which threw light on his personal convictions. "It is in reality the probity and intensity with which the master has carried out his work by which men are dominated, and it is his method of overcoming difficulties, not of evading them, which gives style, breadth, and becoming mystery to his execution."

His own development has been remarkably consistent with these ideas. After the natural romanticism of the early years he affirms himself more and more a realist. It is not merely that he looks to the visible world to provide him with subjects, and paints almost entirely with his motive before him, but also that he becomes less fanciful and unusual in outlook, and more and more absorbed in simple, unemphatic statement of his subject. In rare fashion the charm, and personal, slightly wayward, style of the early nineties has been stiffened, strengthened, enriched, by an ever closer search for detail, structure, and character. It seems a reversal of the usual process. In Rembrandt, for example, a long period of detailed and somewhat prosaic description of features, stuffs, and objects of all kinds—an apprenticeship of eye and hand—has to be traversed before a personal vision, style, and synthetic power emerge. In Velasquez, too, the movement is from hard, careful definition of form to greater ease, breadth, and simplicity. With Mr. Rothenstein it would appear that a sense of danger—of slightness, of facility of handling, and of surface charm in contemporary work—aroused an artistic conscience, which has made him in growing measure severe with himself, and with his talent. During the last thirty years styles, influences, and experiments in the art of painting, have followed one another with bewildering rapidity, and most artists have been absorbed in manner of expression, in decorative and abstract qualities of design ; but Mr. Rothenstein has been more interested in the content than the outer form, or in the handling of his material. He has never looked upon the world as mere subject-matter for an engaging arabesque, nor as a collection of shapes and volumes to be æsthetically related to one another without regard to the functions in human existence of the objects which gave rise to such shapes. Human existence has always appeared to him too fascinating to be disregarded in this way. To record his own experience, to watch and describe the flow of contemporary life as it revealed itself in face, gesture, dress, houses, wagons, and in all things made and shaped by men for their use and pleasure : this has seemed so constantly worth while, so insistent in demand for expression, that pure design, or delight in surface qualities and felicitous fragments of handling have made little claims on his energies. This suggests the born portrait painter, and portraiture does form the backbone of his production. His portraits are not arrangements first and foremost—they are like particular people, as his landscapes are like particular places, at particular seasons, with their local characteristics emphasised, not generalised.

This likeness, this keen interest in the particular, is what the normal human being has always asked from portraiture, and to satisfy constant and normal human demands would, I think, appeal to Mr. Rothenstein as a more honourable task for the artist than to stimulate æsthetic sensations in a few specially sensitive individuals. But the corporeal aspect which he strives to realise so closely is not that to be seen at a glance by the passer by or the casual acquaintance. It goes deeper, dwells on the forms, searches for meanings, for correspondences and harmonies, and looks above all for the spirit, the vitality which has moulded them. It is this comprehension of living character, and sympathy with the ideas and ideals visible in his sitters, which has made possible the remarkable succession of portraits of intellectual and artistic figures of his day. Bernard Shaw, Max Müller, Menzel, Legros, Rodin, Verlaine, Walter Pater, Henley, Alice Meynell, George Gissing, Dowson and Beardsley, were among his earlier sitters, and since then an astonishing number of younger writers, artists, and scientists, have been added to the roll. The only modern parallel for such a series is to be found in G. F. Watts' records of his contemporaries. Yet neither Watts nor Mr. Rothenstein are professional portrait painters ; and, indeed, it seems probable that no professional portrait painter, jaded by the execution of commissions in which he has little choice or interest, could have built up such a series of disinterested documents of the intellectual life of a period. The power of becoming absorbed in the character of a sitter, of sinking rather than emphasising the personality of the painter, is one of the rarest qualities among artists to-day. The general tide of interest among painters has flowed recently in the contrary direction, towards rhythmic design, and decorative simplification. And in the general enthusiasm for these great qualities, the portrait which aims at being a genuine record of a sitter has been left largely to the photographer and the routine painter.

A grave respect for the subject, for the concrete, visible, world, combined with a faith that the sincere and thoughtful representation of its most characteristic aspects, untrammelled by conscious æsthetic predisposition or formula, will best express the spirit of life, and so the artist's share in it—this is the point of view of Northern European, as opposed to

# WILLIAM ROTHENSTEIN

Mediterranean art, and Mr. Rothenstein evidently shares it. He has commented on the tendency in many English artists to seek inspiration from pictures rather than from nature, and on the fact that Holbein, Van Eyck or Dürer are rarely chosen as exemplars. This is not to say that he would, as critic, place the Northern above the Southern, for he holds that the Italian is the greatest of European Schools of Painting, but it does suggest that his own innate tendencies find their best nourishment and support in these Northern realists and lovers of character. Given the conviction that art has its springs deep in the racial life, that it is not an activity apart, but is at one with and supported by other human activities, there follows respect for the native grown, slowly built up tradition, divorced from which the individual's skill and effort lose their full weight and meaning. Samuel Butler showed that ideas are only pregnant in conjunction when they are not too distant from one another, not " fetched from too far " to be capable of fusion and unity, and that " great " thoughts only present themselves when smaller and nearer thoughts have been grasped and welded together. The hybrid nature of Italianised Flemish and Dutch painting is an example of such lack of fusion. Mr. Rothenstein's art has moved steadily towards contact with the firmly rooted and traditional, and towards the native English tradition in particular. He is alert and responsive to other European ideas and culture, and has an especial sympathy with Eastern thought, but he seems to say, " Here is a proved weapon ready to hand, forged by generations of workers : why throw it away in a search for a fresh one, or in imitation of others ? " Varying the metaphor, Hogarth, Rowlandson, Gainsborough, Constable, Turner, Madox Brown, Charles Keene, are streams which have created a channel in which English pictorial thought flows most easily, and with the least resistance. English art has usually kept near to actual life, loves character, and natural drama, while French art tends towards greater generalisation, style and abstraction—why not respect this difference ? Revolution means waste of energy at best, and is disastrous when merely fretful or without conviction of its necessity. It is the artist's duty to express himself as fully and freely as he can, and therefore with the least possible loss by friction, or needless and far-fetched experiment. Some such general ideas may, I think, be found underlying Mr. Rothenstein's development which we may now follow in greater particularity.

Mr. Rothenstein was born at Bradford in 1872, and came to London in 1888 to commence his training under Professor Legros, at the Slade School. He had drawn with zest from childhood, and his instinct and choice were surely right in leading him to the one place in England where the serious rendering of form in figure draughtsmanship was pursued with complete singleness of purpose. Unfortunately, by 1888 Legros was beginning to feel the weight of years and the strain of continued teaching, and could spare less energy for personal contact with his students ; in consequence the enthusiasm which he had inspired in the school was on the wane. Two years spent entirely in the antique room was a chilling trial for a young student eager for the expression of life and character, and Mr. Rothenstein went on to Paris. For Legros' fine taste and severe academic standard he has always kept his respect, and the Slade tradition of firm, direct drawing no doubt helped to form his method.

In Paris he worked assiduously at Julien's, and met Charles Conder, whose charm of personality and whose delicate talent—fundamentally different from his own—he so much admired. He explored French literature as well as art, knew Verlaine, and Edmond de Goncourt, and became a leading figure among his contemporaries by reason of his eagerness, wit, and ripe critical intelligence.

Returning to London, Mr. Rothenstein commenced exhibiting at once, sending two portrait studies to the New English Art Club in 1893. For the next few years drawings rather than paintings show best the natural bent of his mind. The " Oxford characters," a set of lithographs published at the Bodley Head in 1893 was the first of the long and still growing series of portraits of eminent contemporaries. Academic circles in Oxford were probably rather startled at the coming of this very young man, fresh from Paris, who knew poets and painters unheard of in Oxford. Max Müller and Walter Pater among others gave him sittings. Brilliant undergraduates were included, nor did athletes, who, as one knows, are not wholly eclipsed as " Oxford Characters " by the fame of dons, escape record. But it is amusing to note that their portraits, which include Mr. C. B. Fry, looking rather like a giant St. Christopher, are less sympathetic and successful in interpretation than those of scholars like Mr. W. S. Morfill and Prof. Robinson Ellis. The best things in the set are very directly drawn, rich in the suggestion of colour in the blacks, and are, above all, vivid in impression of character. Indeed, the whole series revealed the genuine portrait draughts-man ; though there were weaknesses of proportion and construction, the keen eye for salient characteristics rarely failed to suggest the human personality behind the features. Technically the drawings are simple, but excellent lithographs, the touch light and sensitive, with textures sometimes enriched by scraping. The revival of lithography as a medium for the artist was exciting great interest at the moment, and at the exhibition held at the Victoria and Albert Museum

# WILLIAM ROTHENSTEIN

in 1897, Mr. Rothenstein showed his grasp of the special qualities that the medium offered. He used lithography not merely as an experiment or a fashionable fad, but as the most suitable means of publishing his impressions of sitters who might be assumed to be of interest to a cultured public—as engraved portraits had been used in the days before photography. The " English Portraits " were published by Mr. Grant Richards in 1897 and 1898, in portfolio wrappers with two drawings in each. It might have been anticipated that, at 2s. 6d. a part, this series, which included Bernard Shaw, Henry James, and Thomas Hardy, in a very varied list, would have been rapidly exhausted by a greedy demand, but it was not so. Probably the publication was never known, or at all events never realised, by more than a few, and a photo-ridden generation neglected the opportunity of buying for a few pence original lithographs of its famous, and soon to be famous, writers. A " French Set " (portraits of Rodin, Fantin-Latour, and Legros) and three portraits of Verlaine were published in 1898, and in 1899 " Manchester Portraits " and a " Liber Juniorum," the last lithographs which Mr. Rothenstein has so far produced. With the exception of six drawings of Tagore (1915), no other series of portraits was published until 1920.

These drawings of 1897 and 1898 showed a great advance on the earlier ones in certainty and precision. Most of the

18

portraits were of half or three-quarter length figures, and the pose and carriage are as characteristic as the heads and hands. The touch is varied from a blunt directness in " W. E. Henley " to one of sensitive suggestion in " Sir Frederick Pollock." The selective choice of the accessories to be represented, or omitted, allows a suggestion of background without heaviness, and the placing of the drawing on the page is carefully considered and invariably distinguished. A fine example of this is the double portrait of Charles Ricketts and C. H. Shannon. The grouping of the two figures at the printing-press suggests the bond of an interest held in common, and gives a concentrated and compact design, perfectly cast on the page, having its focus in the expressive hands and faces. The qualities of ease, and style, distinguished these from most drawings of their day. They were not the result of laborious measurements and repeated corrections, the quick sweep of the hand on stone or paper assured a rhythm which saved them from " still life " inanimate description ; they were not " painted " drawings, but deliberate point work, and each drawing was a recognisable Rothenstein.

Now let us turn to Mr. Rothenstein's paintings. It is interesting to note that his academic training had been entirely in draughtsmanship ; I believe that he never painted a figure from life in the schools of London or Paris. He learned painting in the process of producing pictures, rather than by executing a long series of studies, matching colours and tones against the model. After all, the latter method is apt to become an end in itself rather than a preparation for picture making, and ignores the question of design. In Mr. Rothenstein's case his early paintings contain passages of tentative workmanship, showing lack of knowledge, but they never have that effect of stitching together a series of clever studies which may be seen so often in the works of young painters. It was natural that a draughtsman should express himself at first by tone rather than colour, and Mr. Rothenstein's early paintings are dark and monochromatic. Whistler was a master of subtle tone values and restrained colour, and to his work the younger painter naturally turned.

It is a little difficult now to think of Whistler as adventurous in outlook, but he, almost alone in England, had painted modern life, not from the point of view of an illustrator, but because he saw beauty in it, and he expressed this with the zest of a discoverer. There was scarcely one young painter of the generation of the nineties who did not feel stirred by the discovery, and by the new avenues it opened up in subject and decorative charm. Mr. Rothenstein's first portraits were thinly painted in low tones of grey, brown, and black, and showed an arrangement of silhouettes, and background shapes, evidently suggested by Whistler's work. But they had always a keen and personal sense of character, as well as of pattern. The Whistler idiom was being used to fresh purpose. Portraits of the sculptor Toft, wearing a silk hat and black cloak, and of Charles Conder in black against a warm, grey wall, are good examples. The Conder portrait is now in the Luxembourg Gallery. It has great charm of vision and handling, but is a very early work to represent the painter and, moreover, was retouched by Conder before his death, with unhappy results. I imagine that Mr. Rothenstein looks back on this period with some disfavour, regretting the influence of Whistler as making for slightness, for suggestion rather than precision in rendering form. Most painters are impatient of work done in a period which they have outgrown, and resent the time spent in finding themselves through others. Whistler himself regretted that he had been fascinated by the novelty and vigour of Courbet, and had not been of an age to undergo the exacting discipline of the School of Ingres. Yet in following his own instinct Mr. Rothenstein was probably right, for it is in the company of his fellows and contemporaries that a man learns best to discover himself, at an age when he feels overawed by the greatest masters. " Il faut être de son temps," and to have resisted the enthusiasms of his time would have been inhuman. The few experiments which he made in decorative style, such as the " Souvenir of Scarborough," in which he recalls the subject-matter of Conder and Beardsley—exotic types of women, with fluttering scarves and a general air of 1830 Romanticism—were evidently the result of momentary reactions and of no deep personal conviction, but they probably exercised a side of invention in his talent which otherwise might not have emerged. " Porphyria " (1894) was certainly an amazingly good picture from the hand of a young man of twenty-two. In its frankness of tone, unconventional placing, and simple, direct, illumination, it recalls Manet rather than Whistler. The daring utilisation of striped pattern on the sofa, and the choice of an early Victorian dress marked the rediscovery of " quaintness " in an epoch which the æsthetic movement had so heartily damned. It struck most critics as ugly or perverse, charmed Beardsley, and set something of a fashion in modish design. The general amplitude, and rich, flowing handling of the picture were remarkably assured.

It is more important to consider what distinguished the painter from fellow-exhibitors at the New English Art Club rather than to dwell on influences felt in common with them. As Whistler's ascendancy waned, the impressionist vision of shimmering light and effect became dominant, but Mr. Rothenstein's work grew more robust, stronger in construction, and kept for a while to heavy umber-like schemes of colour, the result of a deliberate transposition of natural key to a lower, pictorial one. The temper of his work became dramatic and emotional, rather than decorative. " Vézélay Cathedral," shown in 1898, is a good example in landscape. The great Romanesque church in heavy shadow thrusts its way into the picture with a bare grandeur of mass which is impressive. The shadow cast by it is continued across the road, where it climbs the vertical house fronts, thus echoing the edge of the great silhouetted building. The eye runs easily over the big spaces of the foreground to concentrate on the centre of the picture space where the square towers and the unexpected squareness of the sky space echo and support each other. Scale is given by the tiny figure advancing from the shadow. The vision is not that of impressionism with its acceptance of atmospheric appearances, it is nearer to the picturesque, chiaroscuro conception of seventeenth-century naturalism. The thing seen is the starting-point, facts such as ladders, scaffolding with masons at work, are accepted as they offer themselves, but the facts are interpreted from a romantic point of view. Everything is emphasised which will add to the feeling of massiveness and continuous structure, and of sombre, threatening power.

The " Portrait of a Young Man " (Augustus John) and the " Self-portrait," which is now in the Metropolitan Museum,

New York, were painted at the same period as " Vézélay," and share its romantic mood. The first canvas is very freely and vigorously handled, and has great intensity of expression. The feeling of personality is given by strong design rather than by description of features, the head being placed unusually high, and the lurch of the shoulders setting up a powerful diagonal rhythm.

The " Self-portrait " is planned with great vigour and simplicity. The effect of the masses of black hat and cloak is almost architectural, from the insistence on the main angles, so that the slopes of the cloak, carried on by the hat, give a strongly pyramidal shape. Inside the silhouette the modelling is fully developed and plastic, especially in the face. Few self-portraits have the candour and lack of self-consciousness that this has, with its striking air of receptive curiosity, and absorption in painting. The picture vaguely recalls Rembrandt by its rich, deep tonality, its lack of definite contours, its rough textures, and also by its strong feeling for personality.

These broadly and loosely handled portraits are followed by a series of interiors with figures, seen with great simplicity, and expressing an intimate rather than a romantic view of the subject. The " Doll's House," now in the Tate Gallery, is a very happy design, where the rigid and repeated geometrical shapes of zigzag staircase and balusters provide an admirable framework, which contrasts with the softer, more flowing shapes of the figures. The picture shows that apprehension of the interesting shapes, and proportions offered by an actual scene, which, in the realist, means pictorial imagination, and plays the part which the invention of shapes and spaces does in a more abstract designer. It is the method of design of Vermeer, rather than of Rembrandt. The figures take their place in the general sense of envelopment and are interesting and suggestive, not characterised in detail as portraits. The wittily intriguing titles of " The Doll's House " and " The Browning Readers " suggest a decided literary flavour, but these two paintings are among the most purely pictorial in Mr. Rothenstein's work. " The Browning Readers " is now at Bradford Art Gallery, and evokes in a remarkable way the atmosphere of security, intimacy, and quiet of an English domestic interior. The choice of accessories, the orderly severity of the room, reflect the character of its inhabitants, and both room and people are as English as Vermeer's or Terborg's are Dutch. If these names come to mind, it is by a parallelism of feeling and interest, not from direct influence. If there be still a hint of Whistler in the design of silhouette and profile, the painting is entirely personal, clear, precise, and substantial in statement. The sweeping curves of basket chair and figure are harmonised with the graceful lines of the girl reaching a book from the shelves, and these flowing shapes move against the rectangles of wall, fire-place, and pictures with fine rhythmic sense. There are passages of real beauty in the lit neck and hair of the seated figure, the form of which is simple and continuous, with its weight and character well expressed. The quality of paint in the plain lamplit spaces of wall, the clear limpidity of colour in the glass and the flower which leads the eye back into the picture with such happy effect, have unusual charm of surface. Such pictures as these were the progenitors of a long line of " New English " Interiors.

A group of small pictures treating such themes as " Mother and Child," " Bed-time," " Preparing for the Bath," pointed towards a return—with a difference—to the " subject pictures " which had been so derided by the " New " movements. It required a certain courage for a young artist to paint scenes of normal domestic experience which had been made ridiculous and nauseating so often by mawkish sentimentality, in pictures of the Christmas almanac type. One's resentment at such stuff is caused chiefly by the " faking " of sentiment, by the deliberate " make up " of a picture in which the components are chosen to provoke sentiment rather than for pictorial purposes. Mr. Rothenstein was stimulated by the interesting arrangements, the harmonious grouping, and expressive movements which such subjects offered. Rendering these quite simply and pictorially, he accepted also their human associations of tenderness and intimacy. The difference was that between sentiment which springs naturally from life and images of life, and sentiment applied to a subject from without. Technically these domestic subject pictures, with their warm transparent browns and creamy tones, leaned towards that English tradition which had been broken by Pre-Raphaelite insistence on sharp, brilliant local tints.

In 1904 the "Talmud School" appeared, the first of a series of Jewish subjects which attracted great attention. The starting-point was quite casual and accidental. A meeting in Spitalfields for quite other purposes led to a visit to one of the old Synagogues, where the impressive picturesqueness of age-long ritual in dim Rembrandtesque surroundings captivated the painter. With some difficulty he obtained permission to make studies, and for several years had a studio in the district. Artistically the interest lay in the execution of larger canvases, with richer and more definite local colour than he had used up to this time, and infusing interests of design with the strong human interest of amazingly picturesque figures and costumes. The subject would have fascinated Rembrandt and almost inevitably recalled him. Mr. Rothenstein had not the backing which Rembrandt's training gave him of a conventional scheme of chiaroscuro, so valuable in giving unity and concentration to a great variety of detail. Nor was Whistler's technique of any avail, that of a unified flow of tone which might suggest, but never grappled with, the realisation of concrete form and structure. Mr. Rothenstein put aside pleasant surface and ease of handling for simple, direct rendering of construction in solid heavy paint, to which a certain abruptness and clumsiness of touch seemed not inappropriate. He certainly succeeded in expressing what had interested him so deeply in the actual figures and their surroundings. The intensity of dramatic characterisation in certain heads and hands, and the dignity of certain figures, are remarkable, and where decorative beauty is sacrificed to human significance, it is done intentionally. If it be illustration to throw one's main energy into the truthful portrayal of actual people, costumes, and places, then these are illustrations, but they are weighty and significant, not literal, but simplified to express emotion. To suggest that they are " literary " rather than " pictorial " is to hold that the visual impressions of drama that we all get in some degree from life can be better expressed in words, which are abstractions, than by the pre-eminently visual medium of painting. However distinct and special the purely sensuous, direct appeal of any art—music, sculpture, architecture, or painting—our remembrances of it do fuse themselves in a general mass of associations and ideas which make up our complete personalities, and Mr. Rothenstein has always refused to separate wholly the different emotions of a human personality, and holds that to cut away all associations from an art is to impoverish and dehumanise what is an essentially human creation. The test for such definite subject pictures might well be—" Could any other art express as fully the same emotions which these paintings evoke ? " If not, their aim is properly, if not purely, pictorial. Then, the very great difficulty of the problem is to co-ordinate the pictorial and the dramatic qualities, and it may be admitted that this is not always solved. In some canvases the success in description has overweighted the picture. There is a tendency towards over-emphasis in facial expression, and to the modelling up of interesting portions, so that some figures and heads remain as separate studies, not perfectly related. In " Aliens at Prayer " (now at Melbourne), for example, in spite of the powerful rhythm of line and mass the three figures are so different in treatment and scale (the result perhaps of too near a view-point) as to break up unduly the feeling of the picture as a flat surface. One of the most remarkable of this set is the large " Kissing the Law " (Johannesburg Gallery). The grouping of the figures passing in procession across the picture is weighty and convincing, while the interior of the synagogue, and the great chandelier, in dim London lighting, are admirably painted.

In 1910 Mr. Rothenstein spent five months in India, a travel project which had long been in his mind. The religious and philosophic ideas of the East had always interested him deeply, and he had been one of the earliest collectors of Indian Art. The direct result of the journey was a large number of pastel and gouache studies, and some large canvases which were built up later from these. They are not, I think, of the first importance in his work, the picturesqueness being probably too new and insistent for intimate understanding. But indirectly this voyage marks an important development. The radiance of light and colour in India, the delicacy given by it to the shapes and relief of figures, made a great impression. Here it was not necessary to use heavy contrasts of tone in order to express firmness and strength. The diffusion of light was so strong as to reveal the most delicate inner drawing, and the lightest, simplest style seemed to be the most truthful and the most impressive. From now onward the key of tone and colour is raised, the umbers and blacks disappear.

Mr. Rothenstein's landscape work had already shown a movement towards light and colour. Compare the " Deserted

# WILLIAM ROTHENSTEIN

Quarry " of 1904 with " Threshing in Burgundy " of 1906. The Quarry picture has something of the dramatic temper of "Vézélay," though it is less conventionally picturesque both in subject and handling. It impresses by strong contrasts of tone and lays especial emphasis on geometrical shapes, and the construction of rock forms. The colour has great character, but is entirely in a scheme of greys and grey-greens. In " The Burgundy " picture the tonality is quite different. To render the brilliancy of sunlight and outdoor values, colour has been broken up, and touches of solid pigment have given a roughness of surface akin to that of Claude Monet or Wilson Steer. This feeling for bright iridescence is combined, however, with a characteristic determination for as complete a realisation as possible of detail and structure, which differentiates the picture from impressionism. The interesting passage on the left, where the intricate shapes of a cart pass into shadow and emerge again into light, is evidently the work of a draughts-man who is interested in concrete objects, and their charac-teristics, as well as in effect. The " Church at St. Seine," too, shows similar brilliancy of tone, with strong linear drawing and construction. Some studies of sea and cliffs made in Nomandy about 1909 are especially interesting as showing deliberate simplification, and an emphasis on well-marked angles rather than on small modulations of contour. The

31

result is an impressive feeling of bulk and square massiveness in the rocks, contrasted with the smooth, slow-moving swell of the sea.

Mr. Rothenstein's meeting with Rabindranath Tagore in India, and their subsequent friendship, led to a series of portraits. A set of six chalk drawings of the poet was published in 1915—" Dulcet drawings," as Mr. Max Beerbohm happily described them, with a new delicacy and precision of line· The painted portraits of Tagore, and a large decorative work symbolising " The Religions of East and West " show a fusion of Oriental simplicity and suavity of rhythm and colour with the more solid realisation of European art. Contrasts of tone are laid aside for more linear design, and large spaces of tranquil local colour. These decorative canvases were interesting experiments rather than complete successes. Concentration and character are more native to Mr. Rothenstein's talent than arabesque and pattern.

The years between 1912 and 1920 were spent in the Cotswolds. This life in the country was a great refreshment and stimulus to Mr. Rothenstein, and he set himself with enthusiasm to interpret the new subjects it offered so abundantly. The continuity of the processes of nature which have their counterpart in the scarcely changing duties and traditional occupations of country folk, impressed him as the

32

permanence of ritual, thought, and gesture in Jewish and Indian life had done. It was impossible for him to look at this landscape, these houses, and barns, merely as varied shapes, colours, and patterns, he could not be content unless the meaning and the human associations found expression too. "St. Martin's Summer" is a study of the personality of a noble wych-elm. The firmly rooted tree, the fan-like spread of its branches, the intricacies of its smaller twigs reaching towards the light, are seen in steady sunshine against a still autumnal sky, and are not merely suggested, but are followed and recorded with the most patient care. In another work, the "Old Barn" has evidently grown to meet fresh human needs, is articulated like an organic structure, and is full of suggestions of life and purpose. In "The Storm," the familiar shapes of house and garden are given a strange beauty by the heavy purple black sky behind it. It is interesting to compare this with "Vézélay" and to note the great difference in tone and colour, the much sharper definition and more searching delineation of detail in the later painting, and to find, nevertheless, in both a similar underlying feeling for massive structure, and for the thrust of a large wall into the depth of picture space. "Benares," midway in date, shows the same feeling for long perspectives of buildings; it is a motive which evidently makes a constant and profound appeal to the painter. Technically these paintings are further developments of the interest in high-pitched, brilliant colour, which commenced in the Burgundian landscapes and was confirmed in India. The rugged surface which is the result of building up touches of solid pigment, and which helps to give a certain unity of texture to the picture, is seen also in figure pieces. " Eli the Thatcher " is an example of this impressionistic technique, combined with a strong emphasis on planes, and enclosing shapes, bounded by definite contour lines. It is one of Mr. Rothenstein's most convincing interpretations of character.

During the latter years of the War Mr. Rothenstein was one of the official artists, and was engaged chiefly in making records of the shell-torn landscapes, and grim but fascinating ruins in the battle-fields of the Somme area. His gouache drawings and paintings are genuine records, where the subjects, faithfully characterised without exaggeration, are allowed to speak for themselves. They are studies in the spirit of place, and the wildly picturesque and fantastic shapes of earth, houses, and trees are not used as the material for further personal fantasy in dramatic or decorative pattern. Bourbon Church, Havrincourt Wood, Peronne, are among his subjects. " Huy," in snow, with its almost unruffled reflection in the river doubling the shapes of the masses, shows how effective a design can be found in nature, the repeated horizontals being slightly emphasised to connect and unify the scheme. There is, moreover, a remarkable sense of winter stillness, and spirit of hour as well as place is conveyed by this painting.

In 1920 Mr. Rothenstein accepted the Principalship of the Royal College of Art, and his return to London offered an opportunity for portrait drawing which he seized with enthusiasm. In returning to the branch of work with which he began his career, he was able to indulge not only his immense interest in people of intellectual and artistic distinction, but also his love of the craft of drawing for its own sake, his pleasure in its actual practice. But he aims now at more austere qualities than those of " Oxford Characters " and " English Portraits." He desires that severity, precision, and strength of form which he admired in Legros and from which the alluring charm of suggestion in Whistler had temporarily decoyed him. He searches for the long, sweeping lines of a face, the essential angles of its construction, the continuity and flow of bone, muscle, and hair, and endeavours to set them down simply and directly, yet keeping the rhythmic line of a designer. Some drawings are carefully completed, others are rapid and synthetic, aiming at a spontaneous " lyrical " sense of the whole form.

Recent paintings show a similar aim of patient research

and complete finish. Mr. Rothenstein works slowly, commencing broadly and thinly, gradually building up detail, and tightening the definition of planes, satisfied only when the picture holds the greatest possible weight of observation that it will bear. He does not believe in so-called " strong " or " brilliant " execution, holding that the simplest and clearest presentation of the truth is the best ; that to paint a quiet personality quietly is in the end more impressive than to force the note or to apply the same bravura treatment to every sitter. This restraint and simplicity of attitude marks his recent portrait of Col. Lawrence. Another work of 1922 is the profile portrait of Mrs. Calthrop, which shows a welcome return of interest in beauty of line and arabesque, and has unusual charm of colour in the browns and golds of the dress. In this, and in paintings now in hand, the use of thinner pigment and more supple handling suggest fresh developments. The severe discipline of recent years has brought certainty and definite knowledge of form, and one feels that a measure of freedom and geniality may well be allowed to enter, which should enrich the more austere qualities.

Mr. Rothenstein's activities outside his own creative work can be only briefly mentioned. He has written and lectured much, and in 1917 was elected to the Chair of Professor of Civic Art at Sheffield University. With great eloquence and persuasive good sense he has expounded his favourite themes of the vital importance of the artist to the community, and of the dignity, stability of purpose, and lasting satisfaction that the artist gains in return for his service. His interest in the arts and crafts of the past, and their growth from the life of the people, and, I think, his own experience of the vitality and talent existing in both village and industrial communities have made him a strong advocate of decentralisation in art, with a great respect for local and national idioms.

Mr. Rothenstein's acceptance in 1920 of the Principalship of the Royal College of Art was an event of great interest. His enthusiasm in the discovery of new talent, his idealism and clear sense of purpose, and his respect for sound craftsmanship, are the qualities of a great teacher. Moreover, his appointment showed a striking recognition by the educational authorities of his own constantly advocated principle that to inspire enthusiasm and confidence in students the teacher of art must be, and continue to be, himself a producer. His professorship is yet young, but instead of the feeling of stale routine which is notoriously apt to settle over academic institutions, the College already gives one a sense of eagerness, life, and reality, which must have important consequences for the future of art in this country.

# WILLIAM ROTHENSTEIN

Nearly all phases of Mr. Rothenstein's painting are represented by the illustrations in this book, and allowing for loss of colour, and exaggeration of lines and textures, they do give most interesting evidence of continuity of development. Mr. Rothenstein's position to-day is that of an artist independent of all groups and movements, whether academic or advanced, though not antagonistic to either. By his insistence on definite form, and construction, rather than on visual effect, his paintings share in some measure that intention of " making something more solid and durable of impressionism " which has been so widespread in recent art, but otherwise he has been untouched by the enthusiasm of Post-impressionism for emphatic design, or by the feeling for volume and space construction which has developed from Cézanne. While admiring individual talents among the most experimental modern painters he feels the danger of dilettantism and aridity which threatens when art becomes isolated from the general stream of life, and endeavours to bring it back to a firmer basis, as one of the fundamental human interests. His own work springs directly from the beauty and interest that he finds in the world about him, and from his wish to record this as simply and fully as possible, with a technique which is appropriate and resourceful, without arrogating attention to itself. He considers that the period of constant experiment, interesting as it has been, should now give place to one of steady accomplishment and production, in which the results of experiment may be used. Mr. Rothenstein's work may be tested by the standard of " probity and intensity " which he set up in his book on Goya. Of his artistic probity there can be no question, it is as evident in his least as in his most successful work. Nor has his early intensity of interest shown any diminution. His difficulties are those of a man who has too much, rather than too little, to say, and of how few painters of to-day could this be said ! Will and conscious intelligence dominate his work ; which accordingly tends to lack the more spontaneous graces of freshness, and delight. The growth of the exhibition habit allows little more than a glance at particular canvases, and rarely more than one visit, and among daring and immediately attractive paintings in a modern picture show Mr. Rothenstein's work does not easily reveal itself. A riper acquaintanceship would scarcely ever fail to reveal genuine and positive qualities. Occasionally he allows himself charm, as in portraits of children, where a certain frank gaiety and equally unaffected seriousness is conveyed as I do not remember to have seen it done elsewhere. In ease of accomplishment and sensitive, expressive painting, Mr. Rothenstein has certainly not yet surpassed " The Doll's House " and " The Browning Readers," but he has never been content to repeat acknowledged successes. None of those who followed him in painting interiors with figures has so much bite and flavour of first-hand observation, or such sober richness of tone. Nor could one find the equivalent among his contemporaries of that fine sense of the dignity of thought and character which marks his portraits of men, or of the dramatic picturesqueness shown in his Jewish pictures. His work has never been facile, or cynical, or slipshod. His grasp of form has grown more thorough, and his colour more brilliant and varied. Indeed, he has steadily nourished and developed his talents, and with great determination has built up an art which is singularly personal without eccentricity, a sincere and distinguished record of contemporary life as it has appeared to an artist of exceptional eagerness and intelligence. " To be humble before nature, to work, unmindful of everything beside, uniquely for the standard of perfection he has set himself, is the true life of the artist." This was written nearly twenty-five years ago : it is not the least remarkable of Mr. Rothenstein's self-portraits.

H. W.

# PLATES

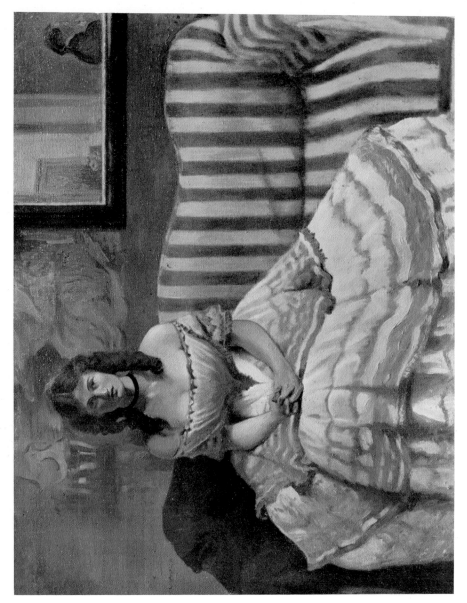

PLATE I. PORPHYRIA. (1894). *Oil.*

PLATE 2.  VÉZÉLAY.  (1896).  *Oil.  In the possession of Robert Baring, Esq.*

PLATE 3.   THE DOLL'S HOUSE.   (1899).   *Oil.   National Gallery of British Art.*

*b*

PLATE 4. THE BROWNING READERS. (1900). *Oil. Cartwright Memorial Hall, Bradford.*

PLATE 5.  PORTRAIT OF A. E. JOHN.  (1899–1900).  *Oil.  Walker Art Gallery, Liverpool.*

PLATE 6. THE QUARRY. (1904). *Oil. In the possession of C. L. Rutherston, Esq.*

PLATE 7. ALIENS AT PRAYER. (1905). *Oil. National Gallery, Melbourne.*

PLATE 8. READING THE BOOK OF ESTHER. (1906). *Oil. In the possession of C. L. Rutherston, Esq.*

PLATE 9.   A FARM IN BURGUNDY.   (1906).   *Oil.   In the possession of C. L. Rutherston, Esq.*

PLATE 10.    THE SOUTH WEST WIND.    (1909).    Oil.    In the possession of Mrs. Weldon.

PLATE 11.  ST. SEINE L'ABBAYE.  (1906).  *Oil.  In the possession of Dr. Jane Walker.*

PLATE 12. THE FOUNTAIN. (1906). *Oil. In the possession of Mrs. Harden, New York.*

PLATE 13. BERNHARD BERENSON. (1907). *Oil. In the possession of B. Berenson, Esq.*

PLATE 14.   KISSING THE LAW.   (1907).   *Oil.   National Gallery, Johannesburg.*

PLATE 15.   PRINCESS BADROULBADOUR.   (1908).   *Oil.   In the possession of the Artist.*

*e*

PLATE 16.  THE RIGHT HON. CHARLES BOOTH.  (1908).

*Oil.  In the possession of George Booth, Esq.*

PLATE 17. MOTHER AND CHILD. CANDLE LIGHT. (1909).

*Oil. In the possession of Asa Lingrad, Esq.*

PLATE 18.  MORNING AT BENARES.  (1911).  *Oil.  In the possession of C. L. Rutherston, Esq.*

PLATE 19. ELI THE THATCHER. (1913). *Oil.* *In the possession of Dr. Jane Walker.*

*f*

PLATE 20.   THE OLD BARN AT ILES FARM.   (1913).   *Oil.   In the possession of Alex. Park-Lyle, Esq.*

PLATE 21. THE STORM. (1915). *Oil. In the possession of the Artist.*

PLATE 22.   WINTER.   (1916).   *Oil.   In the possession of Asa Lingard, Esq.*

PLATE 23.   INTERIOR OF THE ARTIST'S STUDIO.   (1919).   *Oil.   In the possession of the Artist.*

*g*

PLATE 24.   ST. MARTIN'S SUMMER.   (1915).   *Oil.   In the possession of C. L. Rutherston, Esq.*

PLATE 25.  STUDY FOR A PORTRAIT OF JOHN DRINKWATER.  (1919).

*Oil.  In the possession of the Artist.*

PLATE 26.   THE LAST PHASE.   (1919).   *Oil.  By permission of the National Gallery of Canada.*

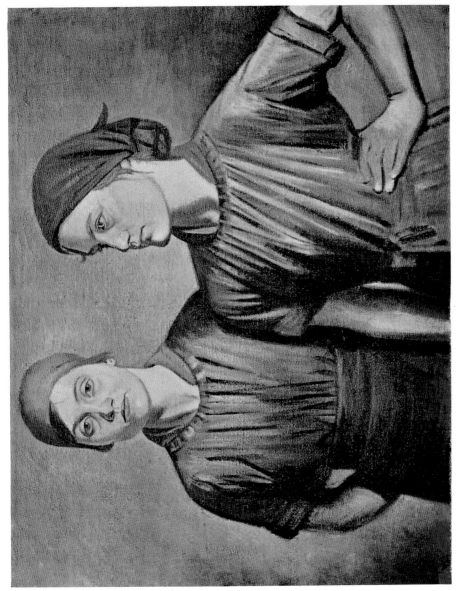

PLATE 27.   TWO SHEFFIELD BUFFER-GIRLS.   (1921).   *Oil.   In the possession of the Artist.*

*h*

PLATE 28.   COLONEL T. E. LAWRENCE.   (1922).

*Oil.   In the possession of the Artist.*

PLATE 29. MRS. CALTHROP. (1922). *Oil. In the possession of the Artist.*

PLATE 30. CHARLES RICKETTS AND CHARLES SHANNON. (1897). *Lithograph.*

PLATE 31. AUGUSTE RODIN. (1897). *Lithograph.*

*i*

PLATE 32.  HUY.  (1919).  *Gouache.  Imperial War Museum.*

PLATE 33. YPRES AT THE TIME OF THE ARMISTICE. (1921). *Dry point.*

PLATE 34.   A. E. JOHN.   (1922).   *Pencil.   In the possession of Asa Lingard, Esq.*